RIDLEY PRESS

Becoming Eve – Study Guide

Copyright ©2015 by Susan Shepherd

ISBN 978-1523286065

Requests for information should be addressed to:

susanshepherd1224@gmail.com

All Scripture quotations, unless otherwise indicated are taken from *The Holy Bible, English Standard Version® (ESV®)* Copyright © 2001 by Crossway, a publishing ministry of Good News Publishers. All rights reserved. ESV Text Edition: 2011

Any internet addresses (websites, blogs, etc.) and telephone numbers in this book are offered only as resources. They are not meant as our endorsements.

All rights reserved. No part of this publication may be reproduced, stored in a retrieval system, or transmitted in any form or by any means – electronic, mechanical, photocopy, recording, or any other – except for brief quotations in printed reviews, without the prior permission of the publisher.

Editor: Nat Belz

Cover and interior design: Nat Belz

Cover photography: Shutterstock

Printed in the United States of America

Introduction

This Study and Discussion guide is meant to serve as a companion to the book *Becoming Eve*. We have developed this text as a tool for the reader to engage personally with the content of the book and with Scripture related to each chapter. While we anticipate that *Becoming Eve* inspires hope and prompts the Spirit's work of transformation in the life of the reader, ultimately it is God's Word that is "living and active, sharper than any two-edged sword, piercing to the division of soul and of spirit, of joints and of marrow, and discerning the thoughts and intentions of the heart."[1] It is our desire, therefore, that the reader dig deep into Scripture as she reads *Becoming Eve*, trusting that the transforming power of the Gospel will prevail.

We have two goals in mind as we present this Study and Discussion Guide. The first is that the reader will engage thoughtfully with the principles and truths outlined in each chapter of *Becoming Eve*. Rather than reading and moving on, the Personal Study and Reflection portion of each lesson will help her to spend some time in self-examination that is guided by God's Word. As she interacts with the Bible and the book, we anticipate the text coming off the pages and becoming an integral part of her faith and life.

Secondly, we hope that the reader will think strategically about how to become a "doer of the Word"[2] as she grows in her understanding of God and of her own habits, her ideas and even her sin patterns. The call to become Eve, to be transformed into the image of God in Christ as a helper and a life-giver is compelling – but it is also counter-cultural. We will not change by simply hoping that it is so. Hope is not a strategy. Instead, we need to ask God to inflame our passion and give us a vision for what might be, and we need to trust the Holy Spirit to begin that work in our lives. But we co-operate with Him by "working out our own salvation."[3] This is our joyful and

---
1 Hebrews 4:12
2 James 1:22
3 Philippians 2:12

fulfilling service. This Study and Discussion Guide is meant to be a catalyst for strategizing change!

We have included a series of questions for use by a small group, should *Becoming Eve* be the subject of a book study. Ideally, individual members come to the group meeting having done their own personal study. That being the case, these questions provide some fresh material that ought to provoke thoughtful and transparent conversation regarding both the text in the book and the Scriptures that have been studied. We would suggest spending about half the small group time discussing the personal study guide and the other half covering some (or all) of the discussion questions.

The discussion questions may also serve the individual reader who is not part of a small group as thought-provoking reflection questions. The questions may stimulate strategic prayer time and an opportunity for contemplative journaling.

Finally, we have concluded each lesson with a guide to a thoughtful time of prayer. We must not neglect the power of prayer to effect change in our lives. Without it, we are lost! Whether or not this guideline is utilized, prayer should have a high priority for both personal study and small groups.

We hope that the following pages will be an encouragement and source of joy for our readers. We are trusting the Lord toward that end.

Chapter One
Mountains & Molehills

Questions for personal reflection and study

1. Take a few minutes to interact with the occasions of the Hebrew word ezer found in Scripture and listed on pages 6 and 7. Considered collectively, write a few words or sentences that describe what you learn about God from these texts.

2. Read Genesis 2 and 3 with Romans 5:12-14. How has Adam's sin had an impact on the lives of every man and woman born since Genesis 3?

How does the psalmist reiterate this point in Psalm 14:1-3?

3. How has Adam's sin affected you? Think, in particular, about your own attitude, perspective and posture around womanhood.

What is your personal response to this statement from page 18? In what ways does it describe you?

> "We must acknowledge the ever-present reality of our own sinful nature. We must be willing to look in the mirror and see ourselves as we really are: women who want to be satisfied. Acknowledged. Brilliant. Independent. Free! And we will do whatever it takes to secure these desires for ourselves."

4. How would you describe Eve's "faith problem", the root of her rebellion, in your own words?

5. Read 2 Peter 1:3, 4. How does Peter's admonition make a connection between our faith and our failure? In other words, when we give in to temptation, what have we missed?

Can you personalize the truth that every temptation to sin has as its heartbeat the matter of faith?[4] To do so, think about a temptation that typically threatens you. What are you not believing about God when you are tempted (what promises are you neglecting)?

What can you know from Scripture about God that can inform your ability to escape the corruption that threatens you because of your sinful desire?

6. Read Genesis 12:10-20 with 1 Peter 3:1-6. Describe Abraham's leadership of his bride during this season of their lives together.

Abraham let Sarah down. How did God demonstrate His faithfulness both to Sarah and to Abraham even in his failure?

What do you learn about God and about obedience in light of this scene from Abraham and Sarah's life together?

---
[4] Page 20

7. We are called to become "skilled and disciplined repenters."[5] Take some time to seek the Lord and ask Him to reveal your sin – the temptation to live independently from Him, to disregard His promises, to be fearful. What well-worn habits do you have of disrespect, disdain and contempt? Thoughtfully acknowledge your rebellion and your need for mercy. The Good News? Read 1 Timothy 1:12-17!

Discussion Questions for Small Groups

What is your reaction to the Christmas scene set on the opening pages of this chapter?

Describe, if you can, the spiritual dynamic in your own home growing up. If you came from a background of faith, what role did your mother play in your family's spiritual life? What role did your dad play?

What other women, besides your mother, have influenced your perspective on womanhood, either directly or indirectly?

Respond to this quote from page 11:

"God's design for gender is much bigger, much more significant, much richer and deeper than a list of things for me to do. His vision for what it means to be a woman who is His disciple and friend is not just about changing my behavior."

---
[5] Page 24

How do you see the disdain for men portrayed in our culture? Give an example.

What are your thoughts around the sociological impact of "gender malice between men and women?" Is this a mountain or a molehill?

Prayer Emphasis

Ask the Lord to reveal Himself as your helper in greater ways such that your confidence grows and your faith is strengthened. Ask Him to help you to see the reality of your own sin, particularly as it relates to womanhood, and ask for a deeper understanding of how that sin is a demonstration of unbelief. Ask the Spirit to strengthen your resolve to be faithful, regardless of the actions of others. Acknowledge your sin and express your gratitude for the Gospel – for Christ, the cross and the power of the resurrection!

Chapter Two
Three Principles from the Garden

Questions for personal reflection and study

1. Take a few minutes to describe your own perspective of "gender." What is your personal perspective about biblical manhood and womanhood?

2. Read Genesis 1 and 2. (While you have read Genesis 2 for the previous lesson, it is important to read it again here. These chapters will become very important for our understanding of *Becoming Eve*!) List the details from chapter 1 about the creation of man.

What additional details do you find in chapter 2?

3. Principle #1 from *Becoming Eve* states that all people are made in the image of God. An image both resembles and represents the original.[6] What aspects of the nature of God are a part of your creation design? How are you like Him (not fully, but in part)?

> Ephesians 4:24
>
> Philippians 2:3-11
>
> Colossians 3:13
>
> 1 John 3:9

---
[6] John M. Frame, "Men and Women in the Image of God," from *Recovering Biblical Manhood and Womanhood*, page 225

Take just a minute to contemplate your resemblance to and representation of God. What is your response to such a profound truth?

4. Scripture affirms the equality of men and women (Principle #2) in both Old and New Testaments. What "proofs" for this principle are offered in *Becoming Eve*?

Let's consider one additional proof. While it may appear that men play a more prominent role in redemptive history, the influence of women cannot be missed. Make a list of all of the women that come to mind whose stories, recorded in Scripture, have been a part of God's plan for His people's salvation.

5. As you think about the movement of the culture toward promoting sameness and becoming gender-blind, how does Paul's admonition to Timothy instruct you (and the church!)?

    1 Timothy 1:8-11 (esp. 10b)

    1 Timothy 4:6, 7

    1 Timothy 4:13 & 16

    1 Timothy 6:2b-4

    1 Timothy 6:20, 21

What general point is Paul making to Timothy as he leads the church?

Are you in danger of giving way to "what is falsely called 'knowledge'"? Is it true that in "subtle and insidious ways [you] are capitulating to the tragic thinking"[7] of the world regarding gender sameness? What is required of you?

6. What do you learn about the differences between men and women (Principle #3) from the following texts?

1 Corinthians 11:8, 9

Ephesians 5:22-33

1 Timothy 2:11-14

Titus 2:1-8

Read 2 Timothy 3:16 & 17. How do these verses apply to your perspective about what you have read and why might that be important in this particular arena?

Take a few minutes to acknowledge your thoughts and feelings around the issue of gender differences before the Lord and ask Him to help you to read, listen and learn from Him as you thoughtfully continue to work your way through this book and these challenges.[8]

---

[7] Page 40
[8] These texts are vigorously debated among evangelical Christians in the church. It is not our purpose to exegete these passages so that their meaning and application are clear. Others have done that work masterfully and we would commend their writing to you. (Most notably, Wayne Grudem & John Piper in "Recovering Biblical Manhood and Womanhood", particularly section II.) Our purpose here is to identify and acknowledge God's plan for the differences between men and women, even if those differences are difficult for us to understand.

7. Go back to Genesis 2. It is important to acknowledge that the differences between men and women, both in creation design and in function, were not instigated by the fall. They were intentionally incorporated into humanity by God as a part of His creation. What thoughts or feelings does that truth evoke in you?

Read Genesis 1:31 and write it out here. How does this truth instruct you? How does it challenge you?

Discussion Questions for Small Groups

Why is the issue of "gender" so important to the Christian? What challenges are we facing in the church around "gender?"

What is your personal perspective about biblical manhood and womanhood?

Why is "image bearing" significant to the gender discussion?

How does the principle of being created equally in the image of God impact the discussion of "gender?" LEADER: Compare the lists that participants made in response to Question 4.

Respond to the distinction that "equal does not mean same."

How is this truth being challenged by the culture (from your experience)?

What new insight, if any, did you gain regarding the differences between men and women designed by God at the time of creation?[9]

Why is the descriptive phrase "designed by God at the time of creation" pivotal to our understanding of gender?

Why is it noteworthy that God left Adam alone for a time (with no helper)?

Respond to this quote given what you have learned:

"It is very important to know that this need for a helper was an expression of his [Adam's] perfect image-bearing personhood. He really did need a helper."[10]

Before going forward, what is your perception of being a "helper?" Write it down.

LEADER: This will be a good reference point to return to after finishing the study!

Prayer Emphasis

Express your gratitude for God's great and thrilling creation design. Acknowledge your failure to bear His image in a way that brings Him glory and ask Him to begin a work of transformation in your hearts and minds partic-

---
[9] Please see footnote #8. Don't get distracted by a debate regarding these texts.
[10] Page 47

ularly as it relates to womanhood. Ask the Spirit to help you to agree with, submit to and celebrate God's plan for gender differences. Pray for protection from the enemy whose lies have wrecked such havoc in the world around this specific issue.

Chapter Three
The Four-Letter Word

Questions for personal reflection and study

1. Take just a minute to describe how your thinking about being a "helper" has been challenged by your reading of this chapter. How would you have defined the word before your reading and what have you learned?

2. How do the following verses, just a sampling from the book of Proverbs, affirm the importance of defining all of life according to the Word?

   Proverbs 1:1-7

   Proverbs 2:1-5

   Proverbs 3:1-7

   Proverbs 4:1-6

How do these verses apply to the importance of defining "helper" from the heart and mind of GOD rather than from the framework of its current cultural context?

3. Try to summarize in one word the character of God as it is described in each of the helper texts. (These texts are listed on pages 6 and 7 in "Becoming Eve.")

   Exodus 18:4

   Deuteronomy 33:7

Deuteronomy 33:26

Deuteronomy 33:29

Psalm 20:1, 2

Psalm 33:20

Psalm 54:4

Psalm 70:5

Psalm 89:19

Psalm 115:9-11

Psalm 121:

Psalm 124:8

Psalm 146:5

John 14:16

John 14:26

John 15:25

John 16:7

Becoming Eve examines just four of these aspects of the nature of God. As helpers, made in His image, what does it mean for you to resemble and represent Him as He is described above?

4. The "Yes, but…" section of this chapter acknowledges the difficulty of being faithful and obedient when others are less so. From Philippians 2:12-16, how does Paul's admonition to the church at Philippi inform your commitment to faithfulness to God's plan for your life regardless of what others are doing (or are not doing)?

5. As you begin to consider the helper nature of God, take some time to really think about your own experience of His ezer help. Your own walk with Him, your personal story of God's help will be important as you prayerfully and thoughtfully seek to become Eve. Read each of the theme texts below and write a bit about how God has helped you.

Psalm 33:7 and Psalm 33:20 – a Hedge of protection

Psalm 86:17 and Psalm 72:12 – an Empathizer

Psalm 20:2 and Psalm 54:4 – a Lifter and sustainer

1 Samuel 16:1-13 with Psalm 89:19 – a Promoter

Are there "gaps" in your faith? Why do you think that is? Take some time to pray now that God will reveal Himself to you in His fullness as a helper.

6. As you think about what it means to resemble and represent God, having been created in His ezer image, what is most challenging to you?

Go back to Paul's letter to the church at Philippi. These verses were written particularly to the church as they faced the threat of disunity, but there is clearly some personal application that is appropriate to our study. How does Philippians 2:13 encourage you as you consider the challenges ahead?

Discussion Questions for Small Groups

Why is the distinction between "role" and "disposition" significant to our consideration of ezer image bearing?

Respond to this quote, particularly as it relates to you:

"What we must do is discover true femininity that accords with the truth of God's purpose as it was set forth in creation and as it resonates throughout Scripture. We must see that the 'helper' design has more to do with attitude, heart and perspective than about a list of things to do (or not do)."[11]

How do you feel about the "Yes, but..." section of this chapter? What did you learn from Philippians 2?

LEADER: It will be encouraging to take a few minutes to linger on the personal responses from each group member to each aspect of the nature of God revealed in the HELP acrostic.

How does your faith – experiencing life with God as your ezer – give you hope for your ability to become Eve? To grow in your helper disposition?

---
11 Page 62

Respond to this quote:
> "It takes a tremendous amount of discipline to live the noble life of a disciple of Jesus in actual things. It is always necessary to make an effort to be noble."[12]

Prayer Emphasis

Express your gratitude for God, your helper. Work your way through the acrostic and specifically thank God for each aspect of His nature and His faithfulness in the lives of His people. Acknowledge your own misunderstanding of the helper design and ask God to begin to soften your heart to hear from Him as you continue your study. Ask the Spirit to do His work to transform your heart and mind. Pray for protection from the enemy who hates godliness in every form.

---

[12] Page 72

Chapter Four
More Than a Row of Shrubbery

Questions for personal reflection and study

1. Read Psalm 91. What do you learn about the hedge protecting nature of God from this rich text? Make a list of the many ways that God promises His protection.

2. What are some of the things that God protects us from?

   Romans 8:1

   I Corinthians 10:13

   I Corinthians 15:55

   Galatians 5;16

   2 Timothy 1:7

   Matthew 6:25, 26

How pervasive is the hedge of protection that God provides for His children?

What, in particular, are you afraid of or concerned about? How do these Truths help you?

How does this pattern of thinking encourage your hedge-protecting disposition? How will it help you to help others?

3. This chapter in *Becoming Eve* addresses the fact that God's protection does not guarantee that our lives will be trouble-free. Read John 17:33. What warning does Jesus give his disciples in this verse?

What hope-filled promise does He provide?

We are protected, shielded from despair because we know the end of the story. God <u>has already overcome</u> the world. Ultimately, His victory is ours.

Respond to that truth personally in light of your current circumstances.

How does this Truth inform your disposition as an ezer-hedge protector? In other words, how does understanding John 16:33 help you to help others?

4. Read John 3:16-18. How does John describe our ultimate rescue by God through His Son, Jesus?

In the person and work of Christ, what are you rescued from?

With John 3 in mind, dwell for a few minutes on the Heidelberg Catechism Question and answer cited on page 86 of *Becoming Eve*. What does this truth mean for you personally?

What does it mean as you think about becoming Eve, a hedge-protector for others?

5. Given all of the above, what does it mean for you to resemble and represent God as a hedge-protector?

6. What is your response to such an expectation?

How do you need to grow? What do you think that requires?

Is repentance necessary? (Remember that "repentance" means both to be forgiven and to make a change, to turn from sinful patterns toward holiness and godliness!)

What will the "cost" be for you as you are conformed to the image of God in Christ as a hedge protector?

7. It is so important as we ponder being transformed as ezer-helpers that we are deeply dependent on the Holy Spirit and fiercely committed to the Gospel in our lives. What does that mean for you as you think about hedge protecting?

Discussion Questions for Small Groups

Can you identify your experience with God as your ezer-shield? Do you remember a time when God protected you from harm?

How about God as your contender? Have you experienced His "fighting for you?"

Comment on the following quote, particularly given your personal study this week:

"The ultimate protection from eternal death was secured by the provision of the Son's sacrifice on our behalf."[13]

Both the book and your personal study offered several characteristics and strategies for hedge protecting. What others can you think of? What does it mean to be a safe person? To create a safe environment? To shield and contend for others?

How has your understanding of our creation design as ezer-image bearers grown as you've read and studied this week?

What keeps you from having the disposition of one who protects and contends for others?

---
13 Page 79

Is there a connection between your resistance and your faith? What are you not believing about God?

How should your faith in God, your ezer hedge-protector, give you confidence and courage to change, becoming more like Him?

Prayer Emphasis

Ask God to give you a clear understanding of what it means to be a shield and contender for the people who belong to you. Pray for a deep and resolute commitment to be vigilant to care for and protect others, in whatever way is appropriate to their circumstance. Pray for protection from the enemy who celebrates fear, isolation and shame. Pray that you would resemble and represent God's *ezer* image!

Chapter Five
Put Your Finger Here

Questions for personal reflection and study

1. Respond to the definition given for empathy: "the God-given ability to redemptively remember and the desire to understand what we have not experienced."[14]

2. Read Psalm 103:13, 14 together with Psalm 139:13-16. How God is uniquely able to empathize with His children?

How does this truth instruct your disposition as an ezer-empathizer?

3. How is your understanding of the ezer-empathizer nature of God informed by these occasions of the word "nacham" in the psalms?

>   Psalm 23:4
>   Psalm 71:20, 21
>   Psalm 119:50-52
>   Psalm 119:81, 82 & 88

Summarize this aspect of our "God who does not stand far off, removed and distant from our agony."[15]

4. Read Hebrews 4:14-16 aloud. (Sometimes verses that have become

---
14 Page 95
15 Page 97. For further study, see Judges 2:18; Isaiah 4:13; Isaiah 51:3; Zechariah 1:17

so familiar lose their import in our thinking. Reading a text aloud often revitalizes our appreciation of its meaning!) How much thought have you given to the truth that God put skin on and walked around in it for the purpose of empathizing with us in our humanity and ultimately rescuing us from it?

Take the time now to meditate on these verses. Respond to this amazing truth and its significance for your life.

5. How do you understand the difference between empathy and sympathy? Why does that matter? (Think about what God would be like if He only sympathized with His children!)

How might that distinction help you to grow as an empathizer?

6. According to 2 Corinthians 1:5-7, what is Paul's perspective relative to his own suffering and how does that inform your ezer empathizer disposition?

7. The empathizing nature of God resonates throughout all of redemptive history! How do you see these truths about God applied to the church today?

What does that mean for you personally? What does it mean for the people who belong to you – those who are under your influence?

8. Given all of the above, what does it mean for you to resemble and represent God as an ezer-empathizer? (Personalize this– resist the temptation to answer this question generally.)

Do you think you have an EDD (empathy deficit disorder)[16]? What does that mean for you? Consider, in particular, the discipline to "remember" and the desire to seek to understand.

Is repentance necessary? (Remember that "repentance" means both to be forgiven and to make a change, to turn from sinful patterns toward holiness and godliness!)

What will the "cost" be for you as you are conformed to the image of God in Christ as an empathizer?

9. Remember that, as ezer-helpers, we are to be deeply dependent on the Holy Spirit and fiercely committed to the Gospel in our pursuit of holiness and transformation. What does that mean for you as you think about empathizing with all who belong to you?

---
16 Pages 104-105

Discussion Questions for Small Groups

Can you share a time when God's empathy and comfort were particularly significant for you?

Do you think empathy is a "lost art?" What evidence supports your position?

Have you experienced an empathy deficit in the church? What does that look like?

Respond to this quote personally (in other words, is this true in your experience):

> "Left to ourselves, we will not exercise our capacity to think about the needs, the emotions, the circumstances of others. It's too messy. Too time consuming. Too draining."[17]

What encourages you about the relentless empathy of the Good Shepherd in the face of persistently wandering sheep?

As you think about becoming Eve, what is an experience/season that you remember that should inform your relationship with others?

What is something that you know is completely foreign to you that perhaps you should seek to understand? How will you "learn the language"?

---
[17] Page 105

Prayer Emphasis

Express your gratitude for God's great empathy for you. Ask God to give you a desire for nacham to become the beat of your heart as you engage with the people in your world. Pray that compassion would overflow from you to those around you! Pray for protection from the enemy who would love to see you relating to others with an empathy deficit. Pray that you would resemble and represent God's ezer image!

Chapter Six
Two Are Better Than One

Questions for personal reflection and study

1. Choose a few of the psalms of lament offered on page 117 to read and meditate on. What are the sorrows that aroused the author's lament?

How do you see the sufficiency of God to uphold or lift the psalmist's sagging soul?

2. Elijah's story, found in 1 Kings 18 and 19, is instructive for our understanding of God's ezer-lifter image. From 1 Kings 19:1-8, describe Elijah's emotional state as well as his circumstances. How did God help his man, Elijah? (If you are not familiar with this story, it would be helpful to read chapter 18 to give you some context for this scene.)

What encouragement and hope can you receive from Elijah's experience with God?

How should that inform your ezer-lifter disposition? In other words, how does this understanding help you to breathe life into others?

3. Take some time to think about this quote:

"To the psalmist who cries 'Woe is me,' God is sufficient. He that upholds all things by His grace will, likewise hold up His people. Much like the strong, solid column that provides stability for the structure of an aging home, the ezer-helper God is 'He who upholds my [sagging] soul, and keeps me from tiring in my work and sinking under my burdens."[18]

How has this been your experience?

4. Has the maxim "God helps those who help themselves" crept into your theology?

What do you learn from Jeremiah 17:5 and Proverbs 28:26 with regard to this cultural mindset?

How is the trend toward self-reliance in your own thinking detrimental to being an ezer-lifter?

5. From Romans 6:1-4, how do these verses affirm the Savior's lifting of His elect?

What is your response to that profound and compelling Truth?

---

[18] Page 119

How does your understanding of this lifting of the elect to "newness of life" inform your ezer-lifter disposition?

6. According to Ecclesiastes 4:9-12, how are two better than one? What are they able to do for one another? (There are several aspects to this mutually beneficial relationship!)

Can you think of a season in your life that illustrates the writer's point – as either the one who has "fallen" or the one who does the "lifting"?

What inspires or challenges you from Ecclesiastes 4 as an ezer-lifter?

7. Given all of the above, what does it mean for you to resemble and represent God as a lifter, a strong support?

How do you need to grow? What do you think that requires?

How can you pray for the Spirit's help for your transformation?

Is repentance necessary?

What will the "cost" be for you as you are conformed to the image of God in Christ as a lifter?

8. Remember that, as ezer-helpers, we are to be deeply dependent on the Holy Spirit and fiercely committed to the Gospel in our pursuit of

holiness and transformation. What does that mean for you as you think about lifting all who belong to you?

Discussion Questions for Small Groups

How did the column analogy, illustrated by the old house help you to have an understanding of the idea of "lift" and "support?"

What causes people's soul to "sag?" What burdens are they sinking under?

Can you think of a time when you lost your perspective "in the terrifying blackness of night?"[19] How does that help you to empathize with and, subsequently lift others?

Do you agree that we live in a culture defined by self-reliance? What are some things that people do to try to "lift themselves up?"

What is the difference between being an ezer-lifter and offering "moralistic, patronizing, let-me-do-you-a-favor kind of help?"

What is your response to the warning that sometimes lifting and sustaining is not easy or welcome – that it requires speaking truth that is difficult and urging repentance that is heartbreaking?

How does your faith in God, your ezer-lifter, give you confidence and courage to change, becoming more like Him?

....
19 Page 125

Prayer Emphasis

Ask God to affirm and strengthen your faith so that you are confident of His strong support in your own life. Ask Him to shore up your "sagging soul" in your lament. Pray for the capacity to be an Ecclesiastes 4 kind of woman in the lives of others. Pray that you would be sensitive and gracious but also courageous as you lift others out of their "pit." Pray for protection from the enemy who would blind your eyes to the needs and heartache of others. Pray that you would resemble and represent God's ezer image with gladness and joy.

Chapter Seven
A Cinderella Story

Questions for personal reflection and study

1. Respond to the definition given for "promoting" as it relates to becoming Eve: "to encourage the growth or development of something or someone,"[20] "a deep desire to see the will of God come to pass in the lives of others."[21]

2. Is the theology of God our ezer who promotes His people according to His own plans and purposes new to you? How have you experienced this aspect of His nature in your own life? Try to be specific.

3. From Isaiah 53:2, 3 describe the Redeemer whom Isaiah prophesied in your own words.

As you think about people who rise to power and fame in our culture, how does Isaiah's description compare?

Why do you think that is important, particularly as it relates to our resemblance of God's ezer-promoter image?

4. From Colossians 1:21, John 1:12 and Galatians 3:26, what do you learn about God's great ezer-promotion of you?

---
[20] Page 138
[21] Page 152

Respond to that amazing truth.

5. How does Jesus address our habit of self-promotion in the parable of the wedding feast, Luke 14:7-11?

Do you discern a spirit of self-promotion and competition in your own soul? How is this habit detrimental to cultivating an ezer-promoter disposition?

How can your understanding of Ephesians 2:10 give you the courage to resist promoting yourself?

6. Can you think of someone who has promoted you – helped to accomplish God's purpose for your life – by speaking truth to you? How did you respond? What did that mean to you? How are you challenged as you think about helping others by giving people real perspective, truth, to help them accomplish the purpose and plan of God for their lives?

Think about one person that you know who really needs to hear truth as it relates to the purpose of God for her life. How might your faith-filled ezer disposition be an encouragement to her?

7. Given all that you have learned, what does it mean for you to resemble and represent God as a promoter of His people?

How do you need to grow? What do you think that requires?

How can you pray for the Spirit to help you to grow?

Is repentance necessary?

What will the "cost" be for you as you are conformed to the image of God in Christ as a promoter?

8. As an ezer-helper, we must be deeply dependent on the Holy Spirit and fiercely committed to the Gospel in our pursuit of holiness and transformation. What does that mean for you as you think about promoting the purposes and plans of God in the lives of others?

Discussion Questions for Small Groups

How do you think Martha Washington's story differs from that of many wives/women in more current times?

How does God's promotion of you from having been an enemy to now being a child of God encourage your ministry in the lives of others?

Do you agree that our culture is marked by our individualism – "looking out for number one?" What does that look like? Are there times when such self-promotion is appropriate?

Do you see this self-promotion and competitive spirit in the church? What does that look like?

What are some particular ways that we can be breathe life into others as ezer-promoters in the church?

Respond to Pastor Milton's illustration of Michelangelo and the great stone slab that would become his masterpiece David as it demonstrates Paul's principle set forth in Ephesians 2.

How does your faith in God, your own ezer promoter, give you confidence and courage to change, becoming more like Him?

Prayer Emphasis

Express your gratitude for God's promotion of you – from orphan to daughter! Acknowledge your propensity to be self-promoting at the expense of others. Ask the Lord to help you to have an appropriate self-awareness, and to increase your capacity to take the "lower seat" at the table. Ask Him to help you to see His purpose and plans for the lives of those around you. Ask the Spirit to increase your ability to know how to help and your desire to do so, even at the expense of your own "position." Pray for protection from the enemy who loves pride and self-importance.

Chapter Eight
A Puzzle of Immense Portion

Questions for personal reflection and study

1. From 2 Corinthians 3:18, what encouragement do you find in the use of the present participle phrase "being transformed?" (In other words, what would be different if Paul used the phrase "are transformed" or "have been transformed?")

Read verses 12-17. Why is the removal of "the veil" so significant to our transformation?

How does that inform your faith? Your desire to be transformed, made perfect, in the image of Christ?

2. Closely related to 2 Corinthians 3:18 is Romans 8:28, 29. What is the promise from Romans 8:28 that gives us perspective about our past?

What is the important qualifying definition given in Romans 8:29 that helps us to accurately understand the provident hand of God for our lives?

From Ephesians 4:13, 14 what is God's ultimate goal for our sanctification? What is His desire for His children?

How does that help you to have perspective about your past failure?

How can this understanding inform your ability to breathe life into others? To be an ezer?

3. Respond to this quote from page 166:

   "It is possible to love Jesus and still struggle with feelings of condemnation. But to do so is to live in bondage instead of freedom – and it is for freedom that Christ died!"

Are you afraid that God will "treat you as your sins deserve"? What hope do you find in Psalm 103:10-12?

Take some time now to confess your sin to God. Ask His forgiveness and receive what is promised to you. Ask the Spirit to help you to begin to think and live differently, to correct your past failure.

Now, move on!

4. If we were to ask those closest to you, how would they describe the "aroma" that leaks out of you? Use just one or two words if possible.

How is that descriptor an expression of the condition of your soul?

Do you see the significance of disposition? From what you have learned, and your personal reflection, describe the relationship between what you do and who you are.

What needs to change?

5. Think carefully about your home. Who are the people closest to you?

How are their lives impacted by your womanhood? Are you a life-giver in the context of your home?

In which of the four ezer-helper aspects of your disposition are you most confident in the arena of your "Jerusalem?"

Where do you need to ask the Spirit to transform you?

6. How about your church? What individuals or groups of people in your church are potentially influenced by your womanhood (for better of worse)?

What "aroma" are you leaving there?

In which of the four ezer-helper aspects of your disposition are you most confident in the arena of your "Judea?"

Where do you need to ask the Spirit to transform you?

7. Think about "the ends of the earth." Who are the people in your neighborhood, office, classroom, parents association, kids sports teams etc. Make a list here.

How does the aroma of godly womanhood drift from your home and church into these relationships? (or does it?)

Where do you need to grow?

8. Think more broadly about the needs in your city. Name a few challenges that you are personally aware of.

How might your helper disposition have the opportunity for influence, for breathing life into these situations? (Don't worry about specific strategies right now – just think in general terms of your opportunities.)

How can you pray for the Spirit's help and His direction as you seek to bear the helper image of God in your community and city?

Discussion Questions for Small Groups

As you think about the puzzle analogy that opens this chapter, are you more inclined toward enthusiasm or panic?

How did your consideration of Romans 8:28, 29 and 2 Corinthians 3 inform your perspective?

As you have thought and prayed about your own past, what impact do you think that new understanding might have on your ezer-helper disposition? Particularly as it relates to investing in the lives of others?

In what ways are you better able to grasp the relationship between "being" and "doing" as it relates to godly womanhood since you've been working through Scripture and "Becoming Eve?"

Does it surprise you that the context for godly womanhood is not limited to homemaking?

Discuss the principles offered to single women with regard to "mature femininity" found on page 170.

Briefly describe your experience of gender in the church. Are you hopeful as you think ahead to how you might become a life giver in the church?

How are you challenged or encouraged by the idea that your ezer disposition has merit for your workplace, your community, the city and the world?

Prayer Emphasis

Express your gratitude for God's lavish mercy and His steadfast love. Pray that He will reveal your sin to you so that you might repent, and respond to the Spirit's changing influence in your life. Pray that God would put your past failure into perspective, keeping you from dwelling there but teaching you what you need to learn! Ask the Spirit to give you a vision for becoming Eve that encompasses all of your world – your home, your church, and your broader community. Pray for protection from the enemy who would love for you to marinate in your failure and feel overwhelmed by the future!

Chapter Nine
The Helper Refuge

Questions for personal reflection and study

Note: The next three lessons introduce very little <u>new</u> Scripture. It is important that you reflect on what you have already learned as it applies to each of these areas. Do not circumvent the "go back to lesson ___" questions. They are integral to your ability to assimilate what you know!

1. Write a few brief thoughts about Rahab's story as it relates to resembling and representing the ezer image of God.

2. How would you describe a home that is a "refuge?"

Is that description consistent with the home where you were raised? Why or why not?

How does your own story inform your desire and ability to be an ezer in your home?

3. From Proverbs 31 what illustration do you see of an ezer home, one that is a refuge?

How does that inspire you?

4. How can your theology, what you know and have experienced to be true about God encourage you as you think about your home?

5. What kinds of pressures are the people in your home, all those who belong to you, living under?

What can you do to mitigate those pressures?

If you are married, think carefully about the expectations that you place on your husband. List a few here.

Sit for a time before the Lord and ask Him to help you to see if you are not protecting your husband, but are – instead – adding pressure and stress to his life.

Review your notes on lesson four. What applications can you make from what you learned regarding hedge protecting those who belong to you in your home? (Recall in particular the Scripture that you studied!)

6. What does it mean to "remember what it was like" in relationship to those who belong to you in your home?

In what ways are you having to "seek to understand"? What is foreign to you?

Go back to your notes on lesson five. What applications can you make from what you learned regarding your ezer-empathizer disposition in your home? (Again, remember the Scripture that you studied!)

7. What are the issues of vitality, health and strength that concern you in your home. (Think about this from both a physical and spiritual perspective.)

What kind of "sustaining support" is needed?

Think carefully about the distinction between considering life through your circumstances and looking at life through the character and nature of God.[22] In the context of your home, which is more true of you?

How can you a) grow in your own capacity to see life through the character of God and b) lift the people in your home to do the same?

8. How can you "cast a vision" for the people in your home? Think about each person. Take some time to prayerfully consider what might be the purpose and plan of God for each one...given where they are in life today. (If you need help, review page 196.)

---
[22] Pages 192-194

How can you help, promoting the purposes of God?

9. What must you remember about GOD as you seek to be an ezer in your home? (See the last paragraph of each section.)

10. How does the text under the following headings give you perspective as you are becoming Eve (both for your own life and for the lives of all who belong to you):

Another Word to Wives

A Note to Single Women

A Footnote for Wives Who Live with Difficult Husbands

Discussion Questions for Small Groups

Talk briefly about the changing landscape of American women in the home in the past forty years.

How does Rahab's story inform your thinking about ezer image-bearing in the home? What (if anything) surprised you?

Do you think Rahab's gender was significant to this event? In other words, can we talk about her life her faith, her choices independent of her gender? Why of why not?

What challenges threaten your ability to be a helper in your home? What makes this particularly difficult?

What have you learned that informs your ability to face those challenges?

To what degree is "community" significant for our growing ezer disposition, particularly as it relates to our homes? What difference does it make?

LEADER: Cover the last three sections with discernment. It is probably best to talk in general about the principles offered. How is the information here helpful as you seek to be a life-giver to those who belong to you?

Prayer Emphasis

Express your gratitude for God's provision of "home" and family. Take this opportunity to ask Him to protect "the family" in America, and especially in American churches. Ask Him to help you to grow in your ezer disposition, that you would be transformed more and more into His image and that the fragrance of your home would resonate with His grace. Ask Him to give you a deep affection for and commitment to all those who belong to you. Pray for protection against the enemy who hates "family" as God designed it and seeks to destroy both the institution and individual families.

Chapter Ten
The Helper Tabernacle

Questions for personal reflection and study

This is a long lesson with a lot to cover. Consequently, there are only a few small group discussion questions.

1. Write a few brief thoughts about Mary and Elizabeth as their story relates to resembling and representing the ezer image of God in the church.

2. What is your personal response to the principle of "headship" in the church? (See 1 Timothy 2:11-14 and 3:2-7 as a sampling of texts that support this doctrine.)

If you are unsure about this doctrine, or frustrated, you are encouraged to do some good reading on the subject.[23] It is important and will be instructive for your walk with God in many ways.

3. What is your personal perspective of the local church?

---

[23] Several worthy titles include: *Recovering Biblical Manhood and Womanhood* by John Piper and Wayne Grudem (which includes essays by dozens of authors, including women); *Biblical Foundations for Manhood and Womanhood* by Wayne Grudem; *Women's Ministry in the Local Church* by J. Ligon Duncan and Susan Hunt. See also articles from the Council on Biblical Manhood and Womanhood at www.cbmw.org

What have you learned from the "habit of Jesus" that has encouraged you?

What have you learned from the "instruction of the Apostles?"

What remaining questions or concerns do you have? Who might you ask for help?

Regarding Women in the church

4. Becoming an *ezer-hedge protector*:

Do the fears and pressures noted in this chapter resonate with your experience with women in your church? In what way?

What other fears are you aware of?

As you think about your relationships with the women in your church, do you find yourself more concerned with their manners, their outward appearance, their performance…or with their souls?

What can you do to ensure that women feel the freedom to be less than perfect, to be on a journey?

An ezer-empathizer:

What does it mean to "remember what it was like" in relationship to the women in your church?

What is one area where you know that you need to grow in your understanding of other women in the church? How will you do that?

How can you develop the art of listening, of being present in the moment as you are serving the women in your church?

An ezer-lifter:

What is the difference between a dynamic and healthy friendship among women and one that serves more as a "support group?"[24]

Are you willing to speak truth that lifts women out of the pit? What makes this difficult?

How confident are you in your ability to deploy Scripture in the lives of others?

---

[24] Page 218

An ezer-promoter:

To what degree are you an ezer woman who longs to help other women in the church to discover and pursue the purposes of God for their lives?

What barriers do you see in your church as you think about women pursuing God's purposes for their lives?

How can you practice the discipline to resist self-promoting for the benefit of promoting others?

What is the risk? What do you remember from Ephesians 2:10 that should inform your thinking here?

Regarding Men in the Church (primarily leaders)

5. And becoming *an ezer-hedge protector*

What pressures do the men in your church face?

Are you more inclined to correct and criticize them or to try to mitigate the pressure? What does that look like?

Do the men in your church trust you? Do they have anything to fear from you? (Criticism, sarcasm, inappropriate regard?)

How can you grow in the discipline to believe the best about the men in your church?

An ezer-empathizer:

Thoughtfully consider the list of questions on page 224 as they pertain to the men in your church. What concerns do you have? How can you help?

What might it mean for you to "walk around in their skin"?

How do you respond when your church leaders make decisions with which you disagree?

How can you grow in your desire for and ability to bring understanding in difficult circumstances in the church, particularly as it relates to men in leadership?

An ezer-lifter:

How might you "breathe life into the ministry and families" of the men in your church?

What is your response to the statistics from page 226? Do you think such descriptors might be true of the men in your church?

What can you do to encourage, edify, lift the men in leadership in your church so that they will not crumble under the pressure?

An ezer-promoter:
How do you demonstrate your commitment to helping the men in your church to become the very best leaders that they can be?

How can you promote their values, plans and decisions?

6. What must you remember about GOD as you seek to be an ezer in your church?

How does your experience of God as your ezer encourage you as you think about your ezer disposition in the church?

7. Take some time to review your notes from chapters 4-7. What additional thoughts do you have about becoming Eve in the context of your church. How can you pray specifically about this?

Discussion Questions for Small Groups

Respond to this quote regarding ezer-lifter image bearing in the church:

> "When one person lives in perpetual sin, and another relates passively towards her, neither woman is experiencing the lifting power of the Gospel."[25]

What do you find a especially challenging about being an ezer-helper in the church among women? Among men?

What have you learned that is helpful?

Prayer Emphasis

Express your gratitude to God for the church. Ask the Spirit to give you a deep and abiding commitment to her vitality and strength. Ask God to transform your heart and mind so that you are more consistently aware of opportunities to be a helper in the church, both as you relate to men and to women. Pray for protection from the enemy who hates the church and seeks to devour her. Ask God to help you trust Him to be the ultimate ezer helper for all of the men and women in your church.

---

[25] Page 219

Chapter Eleven
The Helper Neighborhood

Questions for personal reflection and study

1. Write a few brief thoughts about this chapter. What are your first impressions?

2. How have you seen "the times change" in the lives of the women in your family (grandmother, mother, aunts)?

3. How have you thought about gender in the context of the world to this point? Have you considered that you have an opportunity for influence that is unique because you are a woman who loves Jesus?

Respond to this quote from page 237 from your own experience:

> "When life together is considered (and I don't just mean married life) the weaknesses of manhood are not weakness and the weakness of womanhood are not weakness. They are complements that call forth different strengths in each other."

4. Think about the "boundaries of your dwelling place." Who are the people in your neighborhood – those with whom you work, recreate,

volunteer, etc. Write down the names of as many people as you can.

Given what you have learned, choose just a few names from that list and – reviewing lessons 4 through 7, consider your disposition as an ezer-helper in the context of each relationship. This will take some time and thought. Do not rush this process. Try to go through the HELP acrostic with each person in mind. How will your being transformed into the image of Christ as a helper and a life-giver impact that relationship?

5. Think a little more broadly beyond your immediate circle of influence. As you think about your community and your city, what challenges are you aware of?

How might your growing ezer disposition impact your perspective on your community?

In what area(s) do you think you might be able to help? What do you need to do to make some progress toward that end?

6. Finally, take some time to prayerfully consider the challenges and opportunities that are present in the world. Which of these most concern you?

How do you need to grow in your understanding of God's redemptive story for the world?

Realistically, what might God do through you as you are "becoming Eve" in the context of the world? How can you help?

7. How does the story of God's faithfulness to His people through Esther's influence and courage inform your thinking about your own part in God's redemptive plan for your "neighborhood?" In what ways might it be true that God has orchestrated your job, your address, your children's school district, "for such a time as this?"

8. What has been your impression of Eve, prior to this study?

Read, once more, Genesis 3:14-21. What thoughts do you have in regard to the timing of Eve's "christening", her naming ceremony?

How is that small detail a powerful illustration of the Gospel?

9. Summarize this season of your faith journey by thoughtfully considering this quote:

> "Becoming Eve. This is the vision that I have for your life and mine. That by the power of the Holy Spirit and the grace of the Cross we might be transformed into life-givers in every sense of the word and in every relationship and circumstance that God ordains for us. Helpers. Hedge-protectors. Empathizers. Lifters. Promoters."[26]

"And we who with unveiled faces all reflect the Lord's glory, are being transformed into his likeness with ever-increasing glory, which comes from the Lord, who is the Spirit." 2 Corinthians 3:18

Discussion Questions for Small Groups

LEADER: For this lesson, it might be helpful to work through these "general" discussion questions first then go into the personal comments and reflections from participants.

Name the women currently having influence on the culture and talk briefly about the effect of their influence on your life or the lives of women in general.

---

[26] Page 260

Why is God's immutability significant given the current cultural climate for women? What does that mean for you personally?

How are you challenged as you think about the vision for gender beyond home and church? Do relationships "in the world" between men and women seem like a land mine to you? Why?

Conclude your study with question 9 and a time of prayer. Think about having each participant pray for another participant in the group. This should be a time of hope-filled dedication to the work of the Holy Spirit to sanctify and transform each woman into an ezer – one who beautifully resembles and represents God.

Made in the USA
Charleston, SC
20 March 2016